I Have Dyslexia.

What Does That Mean?

By Shelley Ball-Dannenberg and Delaney Dannenberg

Illustrated by Erika Jessop

ISBN: 1-4392-3679-8

ISBN-13: 9781439236796

LCCN: 2009903520

Visit www.booksurge.com to order additional copies.

Dedication

To my family: D, D & L.
You make my dreams come true.
Love, S

To Mrs. H:
Thanks for teaching me to read.
Love, D

To Grammy and Bapa:
Whose support helped make
completing this project a reality.
Thanks!

My name is Delaney. I have dyslexia.

That means that my brain works differently than other kids' brains.

Some of the wires in my brain are not connected right, and my brain does not process words and sounds correctly.

My daddy has the same kind of wiring in his brain, too.

Dyslexia runs in families.

Before I knew that I had dyslexia, I thought that I was dumb.

I was afraid that I would be held back in school and not get to move on with my friends.

Now I know that I am very smart and talented.
I know that I just learn differently.

In Kindergarten, learning letters and letter sounds was impossible for me! I did not understand sounds and words, but learning seemed so easy for my friends.

I loved my teacher and my school, but I felt different from everyone else in my class.

My teacher tried to help me. She would spend extra time with me, and I would practice words on cards. Nothing seemed to work! I just didn't get it.

In first grade, all of my friends were starting to read.

I was just guessing at my words. The pictures on the pages gave me clues about the story, and I would make up the rest.

Spelling was *SO* hard for me, too. No matter how much I studied, I just couldn't remember the words for the test.

Writing paragraphs was the worst. I had interesting ideas, but somehow the words got all jumbled up on the paper.

So now, instead of writing, I tell someone what I want to say, and they write it down or type it for me.

Homework time was the worst part of the day for me.
Compared to my friends, it took me forever to finish the
assignments. My mom would try to help, but I would
get frustrated and angry with her.

My teacher and my mom have worked out a system to help me with homework. At least now it's not complete torture!

Sometimes I only do half of the problems, or my mom reads the questions and I tell her the answers instead of having to write everything down on the paper.

I really love math because there are not as many
words to worry about, but memorizing math facts
has been tricky. Instead, I use a number line or a
calculator to help me with math work.

My teachers know that I am dyslexic. They realize that
I need extra time to think or extra time to do my work,
AND I get to listen to books and stories on my iPod or
my computer.

I have a tutor who is teaching me to sound out words and how to spell words correctly.

She has special training in teaching kids with dyslexia.

Tutoring is really fun because I get to learn letters and sounds by using all of my senses: sight, smell, taste, touch, and hearing. I write letters and words in sand or shaving cream. I build words using tiles, or I count syllables by tapping out the word on my arm. Sometimes I even write huge letters in the air with my finger.

My teachers and my tutor are a team. So what I learn in tutoring, I get to use in school.

It will probably take me two years to catch up to my friends in reading, writing, and spelling, but that is O.K. because I have special talents in other areas.

I am really talented in art. I can see completed pictures in my brain, so my drawings are very detailed and specific.

Designing contraptions is also a specialty of mine.
Once I built my mom a "plant pull." I attached an old
bike handle to a boogie board so that she could move
heavy pots around the yard. My mom says that I have
a special ability to create something from nothing!

17

I love getting my hands dirty and sculpting clay. I
create animals, clay pots, and bowls.

You should see me ride a horse! I ride Remington.
Someday I will enter and win jumping competitions!

Because I am really good at understanding other people's feelings, my friends always come to me for help in solving their problems. My mom calls me "The Peacemaker."

Now I know that I am very smart and talented. I just learn differently.

I know that I will be dyslexic for my whole life, but with help from my parents, my teachers, and my tutor, I will do well in school.

When I grow up, I can be whatever I want to be: an artist, a policewoman, or even a horseback riding trainer.

I am dyslexic, and I am special.

What is dyslexia?

Dyslexia is a neurologically-based, language processing disorder that makes it extremely difficult to learn to read, write and spell. Dyslexia runs in families.

Symptoms may include:

Delayed speech
Mixing up sounds or syllables in long words
Terrible spelling
Slow, choppy, inaccurate reading
Guessing at words based on shape or context clues
Difficulty memorizing the alphabet, math facts, or phone number
Letter and number reversals continuing beyond first grade
Cramped or illegible handwriting

For more information about dyslexia visit:

Dyslexia Testing & Information Services, LLC- www.dtisinfo.com
Bright Solutions for Dyslexia, Inc.- www.brightsolutions.us
LD Online- www.Ldonline.org
The International Dyslexia Association- www.interdys.org

About the Authors

Shelley Ball-Dannenberg and her daughter Delaney live in Ohio with Delaney's dad and brother. Shelley is a Certified Dyslexia Testing Specialist and the owner of Dyslexia Testing & Information Services, LLC. Her mission is to raise awareness about dyslexia.

Delaney loves school, and she continues tutoring for her dyslexia. Delaney enjoys riding horses, art, pottery, and spending time outside with her brother and her friends.

About the Illustrator

Erika Jessop is a painter and illustrator from central Nebraska. She lives with her husband in Colorado, where she keeps busy with book projects and creating custom paintings for families all over the world.

www.erikajessop.com

Made in the USA
San Bernardino, CA
02 December 2018